Vantage Point

Other titles available in the High Tide Disability Series:

An Introduction to Mental Retardation and Developmental Disabilities

Functional Assessment & Intervention: A Guide to Understanding Problem Behavior

Home Maintenance for Residential Service Providers

Human Rights Committees: Keeping Organizations on Course

Service and Support Agreements: The Foundation for Futures Planning

The Exemplar Employee: Rewarding and Recognizing Outstanding Direct Contact Employees

The Lillie Leapit Award: Using Organizational Symbols to Facilitate Employee Recognition

Medical Issues for Adults with Mental Retardation / Developmental Disabilities

Variable Pay: Aligning Employee Compensation with Organizational Goals

The High Tide Disability Series |

The *High Tide Disability Series* was designed with the goal of present-ing a broad range of essential topics to people working in the field of disabilities. These handbooks are not meant as dissertations or hypo-thetical discussions of untested ideas. They are practical, nuts-and-bolts guides to help you serve and support people with disabilities so that they might live richer, fuller lives.

No group is more vulnerable than individuals who have develop-mental and mental disabilities. And the people working to help realize their potential and improve their opportunities need and deserve a great deal of support. The *High Tide Disability Series* was begun in that spirit.

The knowledge and expertise of professionals around the country is a tremendous resource. The practical advice and wisdom they offer is shared in these handbooks. What works? What doesn't? and Why?

We at High Tide Press believe strongly in the value of serving and assisting people with disabilities. An integral part of achieving their outcomes is the education and development of professionals like you.

Art Dykstra
Publisher

Vantage Point

A Dynamic Approach to Employee Orientation

George Suess

with Jim Heikkinen

High Tide Press
2002

HIGH TIDE DISABILITY SERIES

Published by High Tide Press Inc.

3650 West 183rd Street, Homewood, Illinois 60430

Copyright © 2002 George Suess

Suess, George, Vantage Point: A dynamic approach to employee
orientation / by George Suess with Jim Heikkinen – 1st Ed.

ISBN 1-892696-21-5

Designed by Diane J. Bell

Printed in the United States of America

First Edition

Contents |

Preface   1

Introduction   3

Part 1: A Recipe for Empathy, Caring and Trust   7
   Arrival
   Bus Ride
   Learning to Use a Wheelchair
   Visual Impairment
   The Power of Praise / Naming Smells
   Using the Opposite Hand
   Texture Challenge
   Multiple Impairments
   Using Adaptive Equipment / Lunch
   The Multi-Sensory Room
   Visual Impairment and Leisure Activity
   More on Praise / Learning Terms
   Sign Language
   Cognitive Development / Employee Relations
   Visual Impairment and Tracking
   Debriefing
   Driving Home

Part 2: Creating a Vantage Point Program   33
   Basic Guidelines

Preliminary Considerations   35
   Pilot or Not?
   Who to Involve

Goals and Schedules   39
   Goal Setting
   Exercises, Activities and Methods
   Develop a Written Schedule

Staff Responsibilities   43
    Vantage Point Trainees
    Vantage Point Trainers
    Vantage Point Coordinators

Reporting   49
    Debriefing
    Data Collection and Written Feedback

Conclusion   51

Vantage Point

Preface |

There are many advantages to implementing a Vantage Point Training Program:

It **helps new employees develop empathy quickly.** Usually developing genuine empathy takes many weeks or months. Vantage Point plants a seed of empathy from the first moment the new person enters the workplace.

It **dramatically accelerates training of new staff.** By offering new employees the opportunity to experience their new job from the inside out, subsequent training makes much more sense. Vantage Point veterans better understand the "why" of such training. This enables them to learn faster and perform better.

New staff realize the importance of quality services. New employees feel the experience. They taste it. They learn what they like and don't like, what works and what doesn't. At a very fundamental level, they have experienced high quality and consequently are more likely to strive for it themselves.

New staff feel "at home" by their second day. They are able to recognize coworkers, know terms and acronyms, know their way around the building, feel at ease with service recipients and understand basic routines–all within one day.

It **incorporates direct staff in the training process.** This approach instills confidence, trust and respect in co-workers that naturally rubs off; i.e., "These people know what they're doing. I can see it for myself." And, involving "real" workers in the training process creates a true team.

Trainers become vested in the new employee. Since staff are going to be working with this new person, it's in their best interest to provide the best experience possible. They invest their time in this person whose success reflects well on them.

Trainers are reminded of basic skills and become role models and heroes. Vantage Point serves as an excellent, "back to the basics" refresher for existing staff. As existing staff prepare for the training experience, they revisit the fundamentals of the job they will be teaching. The emphasis on demonstration requires them to be extraordinary role models. The staff set the standard of performance to which others will aspire. They become heroes as well as role models the organization can be proud of. These are roles they maintain well into the future.

New staff are more quickly assimilated into the program team. Instead of waiting days or weeks to get their feet wet, Vantage Point allows new employees to "dive right in and start to swim" in the team process.

Vantage Point sets the tone for the employment relationship. Later in this monograph, you will learn about debriefing. It may come as no surprise that "gratitude" so often permeates the feedback that is received. Employee after employee raves about the power of the experience. And they are thankful for it. Comments like "this is the most unique experience I've ever had. Thank you." "No one's ever treated me this way at any other job." And, "I can't believe you dedicated an entire day to me. I've never felt so privileged" are quite common. What a great way to begin an employment relationship. What a tone it sets for the future. This is a great day for the new employee and an even greater day for the organization.

Introduction |

The experience chronicled in the first part of this monograph is one example of a Vantage Point experience. The setting is a day program for adults with severe, profound and multiple developmental disabilities. Vantage Point orientation programs have been effectively adapted to many settings, such as vocational rehabilitation, residential and preschool settings, as well as support areas such as transportation services. In fact, it can be adapted to any work setting. For example, what if the first thing a new loan officer at a bank was asked to do was to apply for a loan? What if the high school teacher's first day of employment was spent as a student? What if the new nurse in a hospital or nursing home spent that first day as a patient? At worst, what would be lost? At best, think of all that could be gained.

Have you ever noticed that when people with very little or no prior experience first meet a person with a disability they cannot help but focus first on the disability–the helmet, the person's appearance, or things the person cannot do–rather than on the person? You may also have noticed that at some magical point in their experience this changes. Empathy blossoms and they no longer see those things but rather they see the person within–the beauty, the personality, all the things the person can do, all the *abilities* they have.

More than twelve years ago, the staff of the Delaware County ARC, located in the Catskill Mountain Region of New York State, noticed this phenomenon. They also noticed there was no way to pinpoint when that magical moment would occur. For a few, it might be a matter of days or weeks. For most people, it usually took longer. Whether it is a matter of days, weeks or months, they thought, wouldn't everybody (the consumer, the new employee, and the organization itself) be better off if somehow they could make that moment occur sooner?

They imagined the possibility of every new employee's first day of employment being spent as a person with disabilities who is receiving supports and services. They asked what if–rather than focusing on duties and responsibilities or loads of new and confusing information–the new employee was asked to see the world through the eyes of a person with a disability. Better yet, what if for one day, for one brief moment in his or her life, the employee felt what people with disabilities feel every moment of their lives?

Some wondered if this experience should occur on the very first day of employment or at some later time. Others worried that new employees might be uncomfortable or shocked or perhaps scared off before they even worked their first eight-hour day. Would that be bad? Or good? One person suggested that if a new employee was just not cut out for this work or this organization, it might be better to find that out right away, rather than a week or a month or a year down the road. Others offered the observation that the very first day on a new job is a powerful day. It can be a day full of anxiety, nervousness and apprehension on one hand, and of interest, excitement and enthusiasm on the other.

What if we could build upon that excitement and enthusiasm? After all, it is that day, the very first one, which often sets the tone for the first few months of employment. Shouldn't every organization do all it can to capture the power and the vitality of that first day?

This inspired Vantage Point, a "virtual reality" that, for one day, places the new employee in the same conditions and circumstances of a person who receives supports and services. Vantage Point is unique because the new employee spends the entire first day of employment with individuals he or she will eventually serve, as one of them, on their "turf," in their daily environment. Although they come in cold, they also arrive open and vulnerable to surprise. Their preconceptions are ripe to be changed or at least subject to become rearranged. Instead of being given a series of little speeches concerning the mission and vision of the agency, they experience it firsthand.

Often, the first day of orientation or training requires the new employee to be a passive observer. Their time is occupied listening to lectures, watching training videos, or filling out forms. As you will see, this recipe for empathy is anything but passive; it is proactive, and it is engaging. Empathy, caring, trust and respect begin on the very first day of employment!

Part 1 of this book demonstrates the power of an effective empathy-building orientation exercise. It is Jim's personal account of the day he spent in the lives of Alice, Jason, Vanessa, Ivan and Felicia. These are five people with disabilities who later became five of Jim's friends. Just as we would ask a newly hired employee, we asked Jim, a freelance writer, to experience the program with very little preparation, and to share his experience. You will likely find Part 1 unique, regardless of whether you are interested in developing empathy, caring and trust, or improving your existing employee orientation, or learning more about the field of human services. His account is warm, thought provoking, and charged with possibilities.

Part 2 has been developed for people who are interested in creating a Vantage Point program of their own. In Part 2 you will learn who to involve and how to develop specific exercises, activities and schedules to accomplish the goals and objectives important to you, your program and your organization.

Part 1: A Recipe for Empathy, Caring and Trust |

A young man stands, wavering slightly like a mirage, near the bottom of a swimming pool. The water is lit by greenish recessed lighting; an expanse of darkness looms above. The man studies his hands and arms as they slowly snake through the dense water, as if he is seeing them for the first time. His body as a total pattern awakens. In this scene from the film adaptation of the play "Children of a Lesser God," the character named James (portrayed by William Hurt) tries to connect, to empathize with Sarah, a deaf woman (played by Marlee Matlin) with whom he has fallen in love. James teaches and Sarah works at a school for the deaf.

Earlier in the story, James had discovered her swimming in the same pool. At that time, he joined her in the pool and they made a connection. They later had a falling out because of his inability to perceive and appreciate Sarah's soundless world. Some months later, he returns late at night to the deserted pool. Immersed in this soundless, refracted world, he becomes attuned to the environment in a fresh way. He connects to Sarah, who is now absent, by submerging into this nearly silent world.

James feels vibrations instead of hearing sounds in the conventional sense. He seeks out a common field of experience by entering the pattern of sensory wholeness found in the warm fluid circulating over his skin. He also finds it in the contraction and release of muscle fiber, in the dance of the greenish pool lights, in his own pulsing blood, in the weightlessness and freedom of water. He has been freed from words. James is no longer thinking about what it would be like to be in Sarah's world; he has entered it!

One Man's Experience

Journalist Jim Heikkinen entered the world of a new employee at Delaware County ARC for one day. His experience is recorded here.

7:50 a.m. - Arrival

I left the warmth and cluttered familiarity of my Eagle Summit minivan. When I arrived at the Walton Community Living Skills building of the Delaware County ARC, the February morning temperature stood at a paralyzing fifteen degrees below zero. I rushed into the one-story, red-gray stucco building before I realized I was ten minutes early. Maria, the program director who was also serving as my Vantage Point coordinator, greeted me.

Nonplused by my early arrival, she guided me to her office for a very brief description of what my day would be like. She included a few ground rules for the day. I was reminded that my experience would last until 3:15 p.m., at which time we would get together for a debriefing. I was told that this was not a run of the mill orientation program. This one required me to stay in the role of a person receiving supports and services for the day. There was a plan of activities and exercises designed specifically for me, and my cooperation was fully expected for the best results.

After a few other basic rules were explained, Maria escorted me to a small room where I joined a man and a woman who have disabilities. The man was sipping on a juice box and the woman was tending to her needlecraft. When I took a seat next to the man, he began making loud noises and motioning with his arms. He was obviously agitated. Vivian, the class facilitator, came to the rescue. Instead of intervening, projecting an adverse reaction to this behavior, Vivian gently talked to the two people and questioned them about their needs. Perhaps sensing that my presence may have been a contributing factor to the consumers' agitation, I was ushered out of the classroom.

Rather than forcing the issue, or forcing an uncomfortable presence on the two individuals, Vivian had taken into account their needs first and foremost. Within a few moments, I had seen in action several of the techniques and guiding principles of the Vantage Point experience. Soon I would be immersed in that experience. I was told I would be going for a ride on a bus.

8:20 a.m. – Bus Ride

I handed over my lunch and my notebook for safekeeping to a smiling woman named Lynn, my Vantage Point trainer. In the vestibule, another staff member invited me to sit in a wheelchair–a hard-seated, orthopedic wheelchair. A bearded man bundled against the weather greeted me at the van door. As he lowered the lift, he praised me on how well I had negotiated the entrance doors and the cold concrete ramp. Marcus, who had worked in transportation for five years, secured my chair and me onto the lift then lifted me to the side door. I felt a little apprehensive as I surrendered control.

Marcus then expertly strapped and fastened my seat-belted chair. Shoulder harnesses held me firmly in place, minimizing my movements for safety reasons. I could not get up. The morning was so cold that despite the blast of the van's heaters, I felt numb. However, Marcus's friendly banter cheered me. I soon adjusted as we went to pick up people living at a community residence in a neighborhood a few miles away. As I sat strapped in place, a variety of people with developmental disabilities climbed into the van, guided by Marcus and two other staff members–the transport assistant Jackie, and the house nurse. Although some of the people moved haltingly and were easily distracted, the staff moved with them, flowing with their movements instead of forcing them.

Being both an observer and a person at the receiving end of the staff's empathy brought home to me the essence of the Vantage Point training method. Witnessing the staff's patience, combined with words of constant, gentle encouragement as they positioned and secured everyone, reduced my discomfort. Their attentiveness and positive attitude dispelled my natural fear of constraint and restraint. My body did not seem to mind the cold as much, either. Despite the slow progress in the sub-zero weather, we were all genuinely cheerful. Smiles and good-natured joking had dispelled the grumbling resistance I had anticipated. We felt safe. After this good start to the day, I was ready for the first "challenge"–learning to "walk" in a wheelchair.

9:00 a.m. - Learning to Use a Wheelchair

I was no stranger to wheelchairs, having worked as an orderly years before. During quiet times, we had sometimes wheeled ourselves around. Also, during several stays as a hospital patient I had been transported by wheelchair. On all former occasions, my stay in the chairs had been brief. Now I was instructed that as a part of my Vantage Point experience I would remain in the wheelchair for much of the day. Of course, I could rise to use the restroom. Before beginning my morning in the classroom, Lynn suggested I take a tour of the series of parallel corridors that connected the rooms of the building. I gripped the cold hand-bars on the wheels and pushed off, trying to synchronize the torque of each arm.

I experimented with stopping, making turns, negotiating corners and controlling my speed. Soon my thumbs, fingers and forearms began to cramp. A film of perspiration began to form on my forehead and upper lip as I completed my tour of the first hallway. I became acutely aware of the change in perspective, of the floors and walls, and of the adjustments I was making in my depth perception. When upright people passed by or stopped to offer me praise and encouragement, I noticed my eyes having to flick from their mid-sections up to meet their chins and faces towering above me. (This was strange, because I stand at six feet). Soon my neck began to feel a slight crick from looking up. I wondered, should I keep my head level and look up with only my eyes? What kind of impression would that make?

After only traveling several hundred feet, I felt different, separate and apart. Jaw clenched, I pressed on. Gradually my muscles seemed to adjust, although I felt strain in my shoulders and burning in my lower back. I learned when to rest. I began to realize limitation as I had never experienced before. Yet strangely, I felt exhilarated as I began to master the chair a bit more effectively. I even felt kind of cool. Subtly, the appliance became more a sensory extension of myself and less a cause of self-conscious embarrassment. Yet as my body adjusted to its new life, its new vantage point from its newly mobile perspective, I still knew this was a temporary situation. I could, after all, get up and walk if need be. And the aches from underused muscles would eventually fade. As I worked at becoming adept at maneuvering around, no one looked at me strangely. But, I knew it was different on the outside for the truly physically challenged.

9:15 a.m. - Visual Impairment

Sometimes, in order to be able to focus on one particular sense another sense must be blocked. Modern day Americans tend to favor the sense of sight. We gather information and feelings through our eyes; we read, look at pictures in magazines, watch television, go to movies or gaze for hours at computer screens. We tend to downplay our other senses.

In order for me to let go of my excessive reliance on the visual and open my brain to other senses, I had to be blindfolded. Giving me loads of encouragement, Lynn tied firmly around my head a blindfold made of a folded hand towel and thick shoestring. Initially, I felt both a little silly and excited. Then, as I was suddenly attuned to my sense of hearing, I began to really notice the other people in the room. I became acutely aware of each style of breathing, shifts in position, shuffling sneakers, the gentle sound of Alice whistling in her supported wheelchair, and Jason laughing softly as he tapped the Valentine he wanted to show me. I heard the fluorescent lights humming. All this occurred in a matter of seconds. Then Lynn addressed everyone.

9:30 a.m. – The Power of Praise / Naming Smells

"Would anyone like to join Jim and me in naming smells?" Lynn asked. I heard enthusiastic words and sounds of agreement. Though I could not see it, Lynn had placed a box on the table nearby. It was filled with plastic tubes, each corked with a plastic stopper. She told me she would hold different tubes near my nose to sniff. I would get first guess before everyone else would give it a shot. She passed the first vial under my nose and asked me to breathe in the odor. My nose and mouth tingled, reacting to the familiar smell and taste of the spice I had known since childhood. Cinnamon. Lynn praised me, then passed the vial to the others. As each of them echoed my reply, we shared pleasant associations that the aroma of pastries, breads, candies, and gum can create. A simple smell had connected us.

There were more challenging, perhaps less pleasant, aromas in store for me. In slow succession my nose sampled baby powder, coffee, pepper, onions, cocoa, shaving cream, pumpkin spice, whole cloves, floral scented lotion, strawberry, and toothpaste. I continued to guess first, and the others continued to follow. I wanted to please Lynn by guessing right, and would feel happy when I did. But, to my embarrassment, I rarely guessed correctly at first. Lynn still praised my efforts and gently prompted me to try again. I was not teased or chided, but I did feel humbled when other participants named the smell correctly. (The shaving cream and baby powder especially threw me off.) Sincere, positive reinforcement in the form of praise from Lynn, and the participation of the other people in the room helped me break down inhibitions to discovering this new experience. Once again I had been exposed to another new vantage point.

10:00 a.m. – Using the Opposite Hand

My head and nose were still swirling in flavors and aromas as Lynn removed the blindfold and asked me if I was right- or left-handed. I favor my right. She informed me that I would be attempting tasks that day left-handed. The first one would be letter writing. I was to write a letter to a person in another part of the building. Write a letter left-handed! I had seen how southpaws have to curl and twist their hands inward to be able to perform the left to right movement that our language requires. My hand ached after just two words. My brain, so accustomed to working in a set way, now had to readjust; I had to re-pattern my usual way of doing things.

Perhaps, I thought, people with developmental disabilities have to make constant adjustments, learning them slowly and painfully to "fit into" our "normal" world. One emotional shift I made through this exercise was away from hidden pity to appreciation of the challenges people with disabilities face every day.

I experimented with the way I held the pencil. With no small satisfaction, I learned that even though I was doing it "wrong," my results were more legible and less painful to me. Whatever works–another valuable lesson I could use. I felt very proud of the four-sentence letter that took me fifteen minutes to write. Then, I delivered my mail via wheelchair. I placed it in a large manila envelope affixed to the wall outside the room of an individual who loves getting letters. When I returned, everyone was involved in different activities. The next challenge to my way of perceiving and relating to the world would involve solving a puzzle. Not with my mind, but with my skin.

10:40 a.m. - Texture Challenge
The sense of touch is so basic to our way of connecting to the world that we take it for granted most of the time. Touching objects, whether animate or inanimate, from trees and water, to our food and clothing, to the paper you are holding or a person you love, essentially brings a sense of wholeness to our lives no matter who we are. After blindfolding me again, Lynn placed the Touch & Tell Texture Challenge on the table in front of me. This finished board measures twelve by four by one inches. Ten concave circles the size of silver dollars are beveled into the top surface to a one-inch depth. Lining the bottom of these circles are rings of various textures and, I would later find out, colors.

There was green felt, yellow hard foam, blue plastic lizard skin, smooth plastic "glass," pink cross-hatched cotton, denim, coarse lime plastic, dark brown sandpaper, brown corrugated cardboard, and a goldenrod tightly woven knit. The boards others were using have circles made of cork, sponge, and corduroy. Next to the board, Lynn placed a pile of wooden objects that are shaped like oversized bottle caps, and sized to fit the holes. These round pegs have smaller circles beveled into one end. Inside each circle one of the textured materials is affixed. So, the object of this challenge is to match each cylinder into the hole that shares the same texture. You can rely only on shape manipulation and your sense of touch.

I touched each piece hungrily, not only seeking its rough, soft or slick surface but also its shape. I would press my fingers into the textures, feeling for resilience. After testing both peg and hole with my newly sensitized fingertips, I placed each peg into its corresponding hole. As I became more absorbed in this sensory game, I began noticing physical changes. My breathing at first became rapid and I felt warmer as I concentrated. Then, as I gained some mastery and success, my respiration slowed and deepened. I "chilled out" a bit. Fear of the unfamiliar and the challenging was followed by relaxation and even surges of joy as I grew more comfortable and confident. Of course, Lynn and some of the other folks in the room who were not involved with their own activities provided me with consistent praise and encouragement. Instead of distracting my efforts with criticism, their praise helped focus my efforts and sensitized my touch even further.

A short time later, I careened back down the hall from a bathroom break to find Lynn holding a box and the blindfold. (I was not blindfolded while propelling about in my wheelchair; there was no reason to unduly endanger others.) I parked myself at my place at the table and spoke with Felicia through facial gestures, eye movements and a few words. Felicia had the most expressive brown eyes I had ever encountered. She was quite amused at my growing competence with the chair. She used a padded walker equipped with wheels to aid her in getting around. Before we got too involved with our unspoken joke, Lynn tied the blindfold on and emptied the contents of the box in front of me.

Felicia said, "Puzzle," and laughed.

Jason was also laughing. "Hey!" he said. They knew what was in store for me. Again I would be limited or challenged to use only my left hand.

11:15 a.m. – Multiple Impairments (visual and motor)

Since the signals that go out and return to the brain from the nervous system are sometimes blocked, distorted or confused in people who have developmental disabilities, manipulating shapes becomes difficult for them. They struggle to "make things fit" to coordinate what their brain is telling their bodies to do (which also requires accurately determining the messages the body is sending to the brain). Naturally, this can be a frustrating experience.

To help in developing this pattern-making ability, occupational therapists use a shape puzzle or *coordination board*. The six-inch by twelve-inch wooden board contains paired geometric shapes carved into parallel slots on the painted surface. The puzzle pieces consist of rounded triangles, squares, circles and rectangles. The object of this exercise is to fit the pieces into the spaces while blindfolded.

Keeping my right hand in my lap made the game interesting, to say the least. In addition, if anyone nearby made a loud noise, spoke to me, entered the room or jostled me, my fingers had to retrace their steps or start over. I ended up holding the triangle between my last three fingers and my palm while seeking out its slot with my forefinger and thumb. I pressed the heel of my left hand down to maintain the position of the board. As I tuned out the outer distractions and fell into a rhythm of sorts, I noticed myself rocking slightly in my seat.

After Lynn removed the blindfold, I saw that the pieces fit in shape but the colors were mismatched. The color/shape pattern was still novel and made a unique, if different, design. Later, I wondered how people whose brains and bodies sometimes fail to coordinate are able to find the patience (and endurance) to coordinate and control the patterns of their everyday existence. Perhaps even eating would be a challenge from their vantage point. With this thought came Lynn's announcement that it was time for lunch in the cafeteria. I was beginning to see a pattern or configuration emerging to this whole experience. I was moved towards some kind of realization. I wheeled myself out the door and down the corridor. The most elemental of urges propelled me–hunger!

12:00 p.m. – Using Adaptive Equipment / Lunch

I wheeled myself to the cafeteria. The large, windowless room was well-lit, with tiled ceilings and rough-textured wallpaper. Pictures of animals and landscapes hung on the walls. The tile floors were spotless. Everyone had brought their own lunches. With determination, and the praise and encouragement of Lynn and other staff members, I placed a tray on my lap, and asked the kitchen worker to microwave my stew. I made my way to the table where my fellow lunch mates were opening their lunch boxes. The mood was convivial as staff members ate with us. Just as I was about to begin eating, Yvonne, a program supervisor, appeared at our table. She introduced herself and suggested I use "adaptive equipment" to eat my lunch. Of course, I could use only my left hand.

When Lynn returned to the table with the equipment I had to use, Jason, Felicia and the others found it all somewhat amusing. Other individuals who were using similar equipment looked on with nods of approval. We were joined together in the simple act of eating. Some of us fed ourselves; others needed support. I poured my stew into a hard plastic, high-sided dish. One section of the side of this dish is two inches high. The rest of the bowl has a four-inch side. The high sides allow the diner to easily scoop up food using the sides of the dish as a barrier to spillage. Next, I got a swivel spoon constructed with a wide, flat handle that is tapered at the end to aid in gripping. It swivels 180 degrees at the bottom of the handle to allow food to be easily placed into the mouth. This swivel action preserves wrist flexibility and economizes energy. I had to keep my forearm and wrist aligned and stiffened to get the best results. It was tricky; I managed to scoop up the rice and vegetables but had to resist the temptation to use my right hand.

Again, with each effort, Lynn would point out my success to others or to me. "Nice work, Jim," she would say, or "You're doing so well at this, picking it right up." I felt encouraged not only by Lynn's direct praise but also by her bringing my efforts to the attention of those nearby. I learned that eating a simple meal requires patience and focused attention. Lynn gently helped me maintain that focus by using only positive prompts. Through their body language and simple phrases the others also offered me encouragement. Smiling broadly, Jason demonstrated how to neatly pour juice from his Thermos into a cup, gesturing with the cup as if to say, "See, you can do this."

Cheers! I realized that the Vantage Point experience includes everyone present. Like a tasty and nutritious meal, all the elements are required and, whatever their proportion, are equally necessary.

12:30 p.m. - The Multi-Sensory Room

After lunch, we experienced a place of wonders, the multi-sensory room. Single file we entered a room bathed in purple fluorescent, or black light. Objects in this semi-darkness took on a radiance, or more accurately, a glow of their own. There was plenty to do to engage the senses. I wheeled to a far corner near a hanging chair made of webbing. I grabbed a small pillow and pressed it to my cheek. Music began vibrating against my face and scalp. An audio pillow!

Lynn motioned for everyone to move aside, then switched on an air generator. An air mattress the size of two king-sized beds inflated. Jason shouted, "Hey!" Next, Lynn slipped a tape of water music into the stereo. Music filled the room from all four corners. Nearly everyone accepted her invitation to roll about on the undulating mattress. I left my wheelchair enthusiastically and seized the opportunity to stretch and rest.

As we lay on the air mattress, Lynn tossed out large and small balls made of foam and inflated plastic. We rolled the beach ball back and forth and played catch. Some of us, guided by Lynn, placed the mid-size balls underneath our legs or we rolled over them on our bellies like otters. We giggled and laughed. These relaxing and enjoyable movements of large muscle groups help to increase gross motor skills. And, the fun movements opened us up to finer motor experiences to follow. The five people in the room were to become, in a sense, neurologically linked as if connected by electrified threads of sensation. We began to explore and to let go.

As everybody moved their bodies in different directions, waves and counterwaves rocked us from side to side. I rested my head on a pillow filled with sloshing fluid and looked up to see a glass mirror ball catching and refracting purple and silver light as it slowly rotated. Yard-long strips of corkscrew foil hung from the night dark ceiling and rotated, shooting off sparks and glints of mirror light. Stars and planets appeared, painted in yellow, orange and white.

A fluorescent red and gold painting of a bull stood in all its ferocity on one wall. A number of three-dimensional, geometric shapes glowed on all four walls: a white, open-ended box; crossed wheel spokes; and two boxes joined by a cylinder that was painted in a checkerboard pattern. A large wall hanging with textured shapes stapled to it (a pimpled garden glove, a sponge, and orange synthetic hair, among other materials) invited our touch.

Vanessa, helped from her wheelchair onto a mat table and propped up with multi-textured pillows, tracked the inner movements of a cylindrical lava lamp that Ivan held up for her. Felicia swiveled in an easy chair covered in luminescent sheets. She peered at fractured flowers through a small kaleidoscope. Jason made tracing patterns with a flashlight in one hand and light wand in the other, drawing our attention by exclaiming, "Hey!"

Alice lay in a string hammock, swaying and swinging like a jazz musician. She was watching golden-orange fish make precise cuts, with bubbles percolating all around them in their fish tank. We tapped balloons as they drifted past and landed on a giant beanbag covered in shiny, purple plastic. I arose, noticing an L-shaped, shocking pink tube affixed to the wall. A sign read, "Can you make the ball go through?" After several attempts, I did. I received lavish praise, along with everyone else, for participation. To everyone's disappointment, our time in the multi-sensory room came to a close.

1:00 p.m. - Visual Impairment and Leisure Activity
We made our way back to our room. While the other folks soon became involved in a variety of activities, Lynn asked me if I would like to make a bead necklace. I lamely replied that crafts were not my thing, but she would not be dissuaded. She said it would be fun and placed before me a Plexiglas tray divided into ten sections, each one filled with beads. The beads came in an array of shapes, sizes and colors. Before I could study the beads for too long, Lynn tied on the blindfold. Now I could begin.

At first, I was determined to follow a pattern so the beads would form a coherent necklace, "looking like a necklace is supposed to look." Holding the plastic cord in my right hand, I moved from tray to threading beads in a clockwise movement. I used the fingers of my left hand to keep track as I worked my way from tray to tray.

My efforts at focusing and trying to impose order on my little creation were, however, short-lived. My attention became increasingly easier to throw off track. A public address announcement requesting some person or giving out some coded message would draw my attention. Jason or Vanessa or Ivan or Felicia would say something or try to show somebody what they were doing. Someone would bump into the back of my wheelchair or brush my arm. Sometimes a whiff of a visitor's cologne would trip a memory. Oftentimes, my mind would just plain drift then return to necklace making.

Determined to receive the praise I had grown to enjoy so much, I would again begin to manipulate the beads. I began to wonder if I was under any time constraints. I attempted to ask Lynn. But, Lynn's voice did not answer me; the voice belonged to someone else, a different trainer named Dexter. (Later on, I was told that switching trainers is never done this way under normal circumstances. But, for the "new employee" it was done on purpose so I would feel the impact of surprise and confusion. I made a mental note about the importance of making sure transitions are explained to every single person–a valuable lesson.)

Dexter told me the exercise would end in a few minutes, and without any fishing on my part he said, "What a great necklace. I like the way the colors and shapes combine and work together." He was right. It was a great necklace. I now keep it in my top desk drawer and smile fondly each time I see it.

1:15 p.m. - More on Praise / Learning Terms

Throughout my day, I had been both a witness to effective communication and a recipient of lavish praise. I enjoy talking with all kinds of people, letting them know how I am and finding out more about them. To interact, we all seek commonality, whether to reduce that first flash of embarrassment or discomfort or to feel secure in our surroundings.

No matter whom I encountered during that day, a simple "hi" or "good morning" or "how's it going?" opened a door for further inter-action–exchanges of information, of experience or feeling. Simple verbal greetings open opportunities for the experience of empathy. These greetings were often followed by warm-toned dialogue that often focused on likes and dislikes, on attempts to gauge how the other person was responding to that moment's experience, or on how he or she found the day to be progressing.

There was no challenging tone used in these exchanges, only friendly, non-threatening, supportive inquiries: "How did the smells make you feel?" or "Which ones did you like the best?" or "Which part of the sensory room did you like the best?" or "How well is the wheel-chair experience going?"

Perhaps the strongest form of verbal energy I experienced was the lavish, consistent praise I received throughout the day: "You're doing a great job with the beads, Jim." or "You're really picking up how to use the curved spoon, good job." or "Hey, I like the way you move around in the wheelchair, Jim."

After a while I began to believe every word and my attitude became open and positive. I could see this form of constant verbal reinforcement working with everyone. Frustration thresholds increased. People carried on engaged in their activities or, on the rare occasions when someone became disruptive or distracted, they were easily redirected to more constructive behavior.

Finding the ability to communicate on the same perceptual playing field as the person with whom you are trying to connect is essential to developing empathy. Stretching my communication skills was the next challenge I faced. I needed to become familiar with certain terms and acronyms commonly used at the program.

All day I had heard people using words and acronyms unheard of in common, everyday conversation. To swim in this particular river I needed to learn the proper strokes. Lynn handed me a small stack of flash cards to learn. The first card I held read *Reinforcement.* Reinforcement is used to increase desired behaviors. The reinforcer can be verbal praise, a valued object, pleasurable activity, or something the individual likes to eat or drink. As indicated above, the type of rein-forcer that had a profound effect upon me was praise.

Behavior is another term essential in learning how to negotiate the waters of empathy. This was the flashcard I held in my hand next. Behavior is something an individual says or does. When trying to analyze a prob-lem behavior, attitudes and mind-sets often get in the way. When dealing with behavior, it is essential to focus on the specific behavior (i.e. cursing) rather than on impressions or conclusions ("He's disrespectful").

The next card I picked up read *Individualized Service Plan.* An indi-vidualized service plan is a personal plan for each individual attend-ing the program (including myself for that particular day). The plan outlines the support and training an individual chooses in order to achieve his or her personal goals. It is addressed each day by the indi-vidual and by the staff working with that individual.

Some of the other terms I learned were *Motivational Assess Scale* (MAS), *ABC Chart* (a form used to collect behavioral information), *633's* (regulations regarding rights and protection), and *624's* (regula-tions regarding prevention of abuse and incident reporting). I flipped through the simple cards, sounded out the words to myself and won-dered at their exact meaning. I sought their context in terms of my experience that day, I could see these terms were essential in order to teach myself and to help those I serve.

Lynn then handed me a new stack of flashcards that would strike a different chord in the symphony of communication and empathy I was hearing that day. Throughout the day, I had observed gestures and movements interwoven with the activities and reinforcements. Now, I would learn to dance the dance of our most venerable form of com-munication . . . sign language.

1:40 p.m. – Sign Language

Many of the individuals served by organizations like the Delaware County ARC who are unable to speak use sign language to make their feelings, wishes and thoughts known. Sign language is a subtle instrument. A single sign or movement can express a complete thought. Adding expression lends feeling to the message. For instance, simply curling the fingers of both hands with palms up towards one's forearms is the sign for "want." It can be made slowly, gently accompanied by a smile, and "I would like..." Or, it can be made forcefully, driving and curling the hands, wiggling the fingers quickly and adamantly with a look of intensity in the eyes and a set mouth and tight lips, as in "I need it *now*."

I practiced my signs with some nonverbal members of the group. They seemed patiently amused by my efforts. They were like musician parents smiling indulgently as they listen to their beginner child screeching on a small violin or beating on a toy drum. Yet the message was getting through: "want," "work," "sick," "chair," "music," "I want cookies," "good work," and "I like this music."

2:00 p.m. – Cognitive Development / Employee Relations

As the staff of Delaware County ARC first developed the Vantage Point program, they asked themselves and fellow staff members what they would have liked to learn during their very first day on the job. "The names of co-workers," was one of the items at the very top of the list. With that in mind, an indispensable Vantage Point tradition began. Lynn handed me a stack of glossy Polaroid photographs, twenty-three in all. On the back of each one was a first name and a job title or designation. This activity reminded me of something from my childhood.

When I was a young boy, you could buy glossy pictures that could be pressed onto a T-shirt with a hot iron. As I stared intently at the photos, I felt the images being ironed on to the fabric of my memory. As I began to associate the images with their corresponding names, I became increasingly confident that these impressions would survive at least several "washings."

By studying these photos for a period of time, I began to anticipate through body language and particular nuances of expression what these individuals might be like to meet and to work with. I began to get a sense of connection; they became less strange to me. I did not have that clammy hands, tingling feeling I sometimes get when I know I will be meeting a number of new people for the first time. I also began to perceive them as a whole, working towards a common purpose. Together they created a certain energy, producing the dynamic interaction and interconnection between staff and the people they serve, a sort of ecosystem. From the vantage point of my wheelchair, and armed with these impressions and a list of names, I set out to find six team members in their "natural environment."

By this time I knew my way around the building pretty well and I felt at ease with everyone. I understood the basic program routine. As I set out, I decided to start with the individuals I had seen during the course of the day at their workstations, offices, or classrooms. First, I went to the kitchen training area. I found Lauren doing inventory, and introduced myself. She praised me for locating her correctly, then signed the yellow legal pad in the space next to her printed name.

In quick succession, I found Carlos, then Julie in their respective offices. Even though both were busy, Carlos on the telephone and Julie at her computer, they greeted me with the warmth and attention I was finding commonplace at the center. Paying mindful attention and projecting a warm demeanor is essential. In addition to creating an empathetic service environment, it also results in a pleasant, productive workplace. A real plus!

Next, I found Sharon, the occupational therapist, helping set up the multi-sensory room. She wiped dripping goop from her hands to shake mine, then signed off on my sheet. I wanted to linger in my favorite room, but I had a mission. After that, I found Olivia bounding around her classroom which, like the others, was equipped with comfortable chairs and tables of colonial design. In quick succession, I found the others whose faces had been imprinted on my memory. Once I had identified each person, he or she signed the sheet, often telling me what a great job I was doing. Some even left a note reading, "Rock on!" or some other fun or encouraging phrase. I felt myself connecting to my future co-workers. This simple exercise had helped me develop a sense of belonging and acceptance that is uncommon among new employees in many work settings.

Finding these staff workers was yet another way of accelerating the training process. All of these Vantage Point challenges taken as a whole had provided me the gift of empathy and so much more. One or two experiences in isolation would not have done the trick. They all needed to be present in the context of sharing the same environment and time with these consumers. Vantage Point creates a virtual disability with purpose, and I was near the end of the first day's journey.

After my sojourn around the building, Lynn greeted me with words of praise. As I handed her my sign-in sheet, she informed me that my day was almost over. I would no longer be using the wheelchair. With great relief, I stood up and stretched my legs and back. Jason, Ivan and Felicia laughed and applauded. Ivan shook my hand. As I enjoyed the simple pleasures of standing and stretching, I reflected a bit on how grateful I was to say goodbye to that chair. But what about my new friends and all those other people who will never say goodbye to theirs? Vantage Point taught me to never take my abilities for granted. More importantly though, thanks to my Vantage Point experience, I will never overlook the challenges people with disabilities face every single day of their lives.

2:45 p.m. – Visual Impairment and Tracking

The final challenge to my Vantage Point day was *blind tracking.* A very important ingredient in developing empathy is trust. Trust extends to both trusting in yourself and trusting in others. Trust in yourself means relying on your instincts and your ability to explore and adapt to your environment. Ironically, sometimes in order to develop this trust, you need to learn to rely on and trust in others, to make yourself open and vulnerable.

Some people would argue that trust goes against our basic survival instinct. They might also say it goes against the flow and grain of historical record and social realities. Nevertheless, you sometimes have to go in blind and be prepared to be surprised, to put your hand in the unlabeled jar. There is perhaps nothing that produces more natural fear than being asked to make your way in an alien environment in total darkness. Feeling my way like a child trying to find a light switch was my final, and perhaps most primal, challenge.

Holding my right elbow in her hand, Lynn slowly and gently guided me out of the classroom. In a calm voice she provided me with precise verbal prompts to lead me across the intersection of two hallways. I felt as if I were entering a busy intersection in Midtown Manhattan. She continued offering reassuring guidance as I took the smallest of "baby steps." I felt the ancient fear of falling or being knocked over rise up from my stomach into my throat. My extended hands began to perspire and tingle. I also felt a little dizzy and disoriented.

Surprisingly, the first surface my outstretched left hand touched was made of cool, smooth glass. Allowed to explore this featureless, somewhat squeaky surface for a moment, my hand traced down to waist level where the cold, beveled contours of aluminum casements were holding a sliding window in place. All this time Lynn provided me with gentle directions to keep me oriented while allowing me space and time to explore. She was a guide, not a boss.

We now moved on from the receptionist/secretary station that had seemed so commonplace when I first arrived. My fingers encountered a rough surface covered with hundreds of tiny, coarse bubbles rising up randomly. As Lynn guided me along this wall, I felt the rough, granular surface interrupted by cold, angular plates of metal that rose several inches in graduated steps like a miniature terrace before descending to a cool, metallic plateau. This metal terrace extended above my head to the top of the jamb then down to the floor. Its surface had a slightly rough, even texture from brush marks left by a paint roller. "Door," I announced, then proceeded.

Lynn's verbal prompts and light touch on my elbow kept me on track and warned me of the disconcerting sensation of encountering an open door. (She guided me across the three-foot expanse to the next jamb.) I soon made it to the end of the hall. In all, I counted five doors–two open, three closed.

All along I was bombarded by a cacophony of sounds and smells: voices coming from the offices and classrooms; the varied undulations of tone, volume and pitch from the hum of computers; the tap of keyboards; and the buzz of telephones. I smelled the scents of people–colognes and perfumes, hair and soap, and the occasional whiff of gum or mint. When an outer door opened and shut, I caught the scent of winter.

Following the sharp edge of the corner, I turned left. Lynn released her gentle grip on my right elbow and informed me she would just give occasional verbal prompts as needed. Although I knew she was nearby, I felt I was on my own. I was determined to rely on her as little as possible. This hallway shared the same characteristics as the first except there was more noise to my left. It was coming from across the way and cascading from the far ends of the halls, both facing me and behind me. The sounds of activities seeped out of the rooms. Instead of being disconcerted and disoriented, I felt I could use these bearings to help me gauge space. The sounds became a pleasant backdrop to the concert my probing fingers made as I took slow, deliberate steps down this second hallway.

After passing three doors, I came to another corner indicating a hallway. Lynn told me to turn left. I did, and my fingers began to confidently dance their way down this passageway. This exploring wasn't so scary after all. It was becoming predictable. The familiar sensations guided me easily past the first closed door. Feeling my way past the doorjamb and frame, I reached into empty space. No problem; obviously an open door. I stretched my hand and arm deeper into the space, turning sideways to anticipate the opposite door frame. But, my fingers pushed into something soft that felt like cloth. Recoiling, I suddenly realized I had pushed my hand against a person standing in the doorway. I guffawed then giggled my embarrassment, and I lost all perspective and poise. The joke was on me. And I loved it!

All joking aside, blind tracking in a busy environment illustrates aspects of both sensory deprivation and sensory overload experienced (at times even concurrently) by the people we serve. Alone it can be frightening, but shared with others or with a guide, the exercise (or the disability it mirrors) can open up new worlds. People with disabilities are, in a sense, explorers. They are constantly challenged to stretch the boundaries of their consciousness. Even the most seemingly mundane activities present opportunities for expanding their lives, for learning and for growth.

I turned another corner. Lynn told me to open the door. A voice I recalled from early that morning asked me to remove the blindfold. Blinking to adjust my eyes to the fluorescent, recessed lighting, I recognized Maria, the director. She smiled and asked, "Well, what do you think? This is your debriefing."

3:15 p.m. - Debriefing

While Maria is the program director, that day she was serving as my supervisor and Vantage Point coordinator. She led me to the comfort and quiet of her office for the final aspect of my Vantage Point experience, a formal debriefing.

So many thoughts, so many experiences, so many feelings. Her initial question, asking what I thought, drew an immediate response of "Wow!" Now, in this quiet place, other words came to mind. "Exceptional, impressive, terrific, potent, yes, very potent." As my initial burst of emotion subsided, she asked me first what I had learned, and then why I thought they do this.

We spent forty-five minutes discussing these questions and many more that I had been saving for this opportunity. The debriefing also allowed Maria to clarify minor misconceptions or misinterpretations that I had developed. I thought about how most organizations leave such misconceptions unattended, and how frequently they lead to further confusion and problems down the road.

It makes sense to take a few moments to set the record straight, to catch misconceptions early on, and to show me or any new employee how important my good start is to everyone. Leave it to the people who designed Vantage Point to understand this and address it through this debriefing. How could I have expected anything less?

4:35 p.m. - Driving home

I drove home that day in a wonderful state of mind. I find it difficult to adequately describe in words the welcoming atmosphere created by everyone, but especially by the people who receive supports and services. I felt that rare sense of community and commonality that is like sharing a good meal with family or friends. All the people working in this place genuinely wanted to be there. Everyone shared a calm and passionate sense of friendly, common purpose. I could sense that people here trusted one another, and I attributed these feelings to their first experiences.

Moreover, my Vantage Point experience was fun in the best sense of the word. I was not merely being entertained but was part of the show, the focus of the joy running through the day. And everyone seemed to be enjoying themselves, too, perhaps remembering their own shared experience of initiation. Vantage Point not only reaches you emotionally, but it also prepares you psychologically and practically for the hard challenges of this new career.

Imagine the Vantage Point experience as a meal. When prepared and eaten with an open mind and sincerity, it develops empathy through real life interconnection with flesh and blood human beings. People who happen to have developmental disabilities invite you to join them in this "meal" that is their lives. They are no longer labels, diagnoses or objects of pity. By accepting the invitation to partake in this experience, you find that they are no longer "less than." You and they are one, equally enjoying this meal set before us, this meal called life. You enjoy this experience as a member of a team. And you may discover a sense of belonging and warm welcome you have never felt before in any other setting.

Most intense, though, is the reflection that even though I became "handicapped" or "disabled" for the day, I retained my essential humanity. I was still a person possessing legitimate feelings and perceptions. I had become a person who could see and follow patterns created by emotions and the senses in relationships. I became a person who could be a part of something bigger than myself, regardless of which label anyone affixed to me. I had come to realize that people who have disabilities have always had their humanity present regardless of my own preconceptions and yes, prejudices.

Through Vantage Point, whether in my wheelchair or fumbling through the challenges of the day, I discovered the essence and the critical importance of empathy. I also learned great lessons about trust–both trusting others and trusting myself. I came away with a deeper, more profound respect for people with disabilities, for the workers who serve them and for the strategies that quality-oriented organizations use to achieve their mission. The experience produced in me new insights, new perspectives, a new vantage point from which I will experience the rest of my life. I will never be the same, and I am grateful.

Part 2: Creating a Vantage Point Program |

Basic Guidelines

Following are the basic steps to use in adapting the Vantage Point experience to your unique workplace environment. They include how to incorporate the basic Vantage Point goals into those of your organization. As you use the information that is provided, keep the following guiding principles in mind.

There is only one first day on the job. This point is as simple as it is profound. Yet, it is amazing how little attention it receives. It is somewhat baffling how one employer after another seems content to let the first day of employment pass without ever attempting to seize the power of that opportunity. Many employers have become accustomed to simply allowing new employees to just get by, feeling successful if new employees simply survive their first day.

Adapt Vantage Point to any setting. A Vantage Point experience can be adapted to any setting. What if the first thing that a new loan officer was asked to do was to apply for a loan? What if that high school teacher's first day of employment was spent as a student? What if that new nurse in a hospital or nursing home spent her first day as a patient? Think of the possibilities.

After learning about Vantage Point, some organizations have

developed programs that are as brief as a half day, or as long as three days. The length of time is best determined by each organization. Begin by defining your particular goals. Once these are determined, the length of time required to accomplish them will emerge. You determine what length of experience works best for you.

Encourage Vantage Point to evolve. Material contained here will enable your organization to establish a Vantage Point program. But, once it is up and running, you can use the information you received during debriefings to refine the process. Also, look at data from employee satisfaction surveys, suggestion box ideas and discussions at staff or department meetings. This information can help you to identify the best topics to address in the orientation program.

Model Proactivity. Reactive or proactive? Which best describes your organization and your employees? The best way to show new employees your organization's commitment to proactivity is to start right off the bat. Make the best use of Vantage Point, especially on the first day of employment, to demonstrate your commitment to being proactive. It sends a very clear message to everyone involved that your organization practices what it preaches.

Preliminary Considerations |

Pilot or Not?

Once the decision is made to develop a Vantage Point program, the next decision is whether to initiate the program fully throughout the organization or through a pilot. Piloting offers many advantages. It enables you to start small and to capture the enthusiasm and creativity of your most interested staff members, while at the same time keeping the initial logistical details manageable. It increases the likelihood of immediate success and creates a sense of anticipation and interest in people who are not actively involved in the pilot. Also, sharing the results of initial debriefings will go a long way towards overcoming the apprehension or resistance other staff members may have.

Unless the organization is very small or there are particularly unique circumstances, starting out with a pilot program is recommended. All other employees should be well informed. They should know that the intent of the pilot is to build the experience necessary to expand the program throughout the organization. They should also be encouraged to supply suggestions and ideas, and to identify any concerns or apprehension they may have.

Use data from the pilot program to address these concerns. For instance, one serious apprehension voiced by a member of the Delaware County ARC prior to their pilot was that certain new employees might resign immediately. He feared losing people as a result of this innova-

resign immediately. He feared losing people as a result of this innovation. Workers conducting the pilot were asked to keep data on reactions to the program. They were able to report back over the intervening weeks that not one person resigned during the pilot period. In fact, they were able to report a seemingly endless list of positive comments. Their observations went a long way towards addressing that person's concerns and preparing his department to replicate the program after the pilot was complete.

Who to Involve

Once the decision has been made to begin with a pilot program, the next concern is who should become involved. When it comes to staff, the answer is *everyone*. Remember, the purpose of the pilot is two-fold: first, to develop a successful small scale program; and secondly, to generate the interest and enthusiasm necessary to expand the program once the pilot is concluded.

When it comes to people who receive supports and services, judgements will need to be made. If a loan officer is applying for a loan it is questionable whether the other bank customers would need to know at all. High school students, on the other hand, might be very curious about a new student who appears to be in his twenties or thirties. Once the day starts, it is very important that everyone stay in their roles. Customers, students, and service recipients should be involved to whatever extent is necessary to develop the most realistic experience possible without confusion and needless disruption.

Pilot programs are most successful when assigned to those with the most creativity, enthusiasm and experience. Effective communication is essential, so the pilot team should also be created with the best communicators in mind.

For the planning stage, look for people whose ideas and experimenting the plan, seek out individuals who have strong, empathetic, "people" skills as well as good work performance histories. The pilot team should include a team leader, clinicians (multi-sensory room, adaptive devices, and so on), other program specialists, and direct service staff. Vantage Point coordinators and trainers will initially be designated from this team.

All team members need to be aware of who is accountable for what. Jim's day appeared virtually seamless to him because everyone knew their role beforehand. They knew who to go to immediately if an obstacle or the need for adaptation presented itself. For instance, Jim was in his first program room for a few minutes when his instructor realized that two people with disabilities were going to have a challenging day. This would disrupt Jim's Vantage Point experience significantly. Jim did not know it, but the instructor consulted with her coordinator and other team members. They decided to move Jim to a different room and substitute another instructor. The team had worked together to resolve the situation quickly and seamlessly.

Goals and Schedules |

Goal Setting

General goals are appropriate for an effective Vantage Point program regardless of the setting. Specific goals, on the other hand, are developed by each organization to meet their specific needs.

General Goals

- Develop empathy, caring and respect.
- Orient new employees to the work setting.
- Model effective methods and techniques specific to the given consumer base.
- Provide initial elements of basic training.
- Assimilate the new employee into the new work team.

Specific Goals

To develop goals specific to your organization, first review existing orientation goals to determine which can be accomplished, in whole or part, through a Vantage Point experience. Next, and most importantly, conduct a focus group of existing employees. Ask them to reflect back on their first day of employment and on the general goals listed above. Then have them answer the following questions:

- What would you have liked to learn on your first day of employment but did not?

•What problems did you experience on your first day of employment that could have been avoided?

•What question do new employees ask you most often on their first day of employment?

•If you could give any new employee one piece of advice or helpful tip, what would it be?

Do not enter this process with any preconceptions. Allow free flowing responses. Follow good brainstorming techniques of openness and acceptance. Be non-judgmental and record all responses. Next, look for patterns and prioritize issues that are specific to the organization and–more importantly–to each specific department or work site. Responses may be as general as knowing the names of co-workers or as specific as how to make a personal phone call. Take into account unique physical plant issues such as where emergency equipment is located. With this information in hand, any number of goals specific to a particular job or setting can be developed.

Exercises, Activities and Methods

This can be the most creative and fun part of developing your Vantage Point program. Distribute the list of general and specific goals. Then conduct another brainstorming session to identify both existing and new exercises, activities and methods to accomplish the goals. Rely mostly on existing approaches and be cautious of being overly creative. Remember that this day should closely parallel any other. It is important to consider that the Vantage Point trainers will also be engaged in their normal job duties that day. Performing an entirely new set of exercises or different activities may not be possible and may discourage their participation.

Certain exercises, like writing with the opposite hand, wearing a blindfold, and maneuvering in a wheelchair were specifically designed for the goal of developing empathy. Other exercises served other purposes. Remember the naming smells exercise? Jim participated right along with everyone else. No different from the rest of the group and certainly no better than any other individual. In addition to developing empathy, the goal here was for the Vantage Point trainer to model good teaching techniques and to orient Jim to a particular routine.

Learning terminology and a few manual signs serve to provide initial elements of training that give the employee a taste of things to come. Having someone appear in a doorway when Jim was blind tracking and expecting an empty opening was a fun and gentle way for other team members to welcome Jim and be a part of his Vantage Point day.

Develop a Written Schedule

Once activities and exercises have been developed, a written schedule of the day (or evening as the case may be) should be developed and shared with the immediate team and as many others as is appropriate. The purpose here is two-fold. First, leaders can share information and build interest and enthusiasm for the project. Secondly, the team can be asked to think through the entire day, minute by minute, to identify gaps, potential disruptions or areas of concerns.

What happens when there is a fire drill and Jim is in a wheelchair? Or if there is some other type of emergency? What happens during coffee breaks or bathroom breaks? What if Jim were to receive a personal phone call during his Vantage Point experience? Think about the types of disruptions that normally occur. Be particularly attentive to periods of transition. Who normally needs more attention or assistance at what times and how will that impact the person in Vantage Point? This is a good time to consider what materials or supplies will be needed and make sure they are available.

Staff Responsibilities |

While the project or team leader has been responsible for developing the Vantage Point program to this point, attention should now shift to the three key players in a Vantage Point experience.

- The *trainee* is the new employee who will be experiencing Vantage Point.
- The *trainer* is the staff person, usually at the direct service level, who will maintain primary contact with the *trainee*.
- The *coordinator* is the staff person, usually an experienced supervisor, who prepares both the trainee and the trainer and maintains overall responsibility for the experience.

Careful consideration should be given to each of these roles. Specific written responsibilities or directions should be developed for the trainer and the coordinator. With the Vantage Point trainee, care should be taken to give enough basic information so as to properly prepare the individual, but not so much as to diminish the impact of the experience.

Vantage Point Trainees

The following letter achieves three goals. It gives the new hire certain basic information, such as wear comfortable clothes and bring a lunch. It also develops a sense of anticipation, openness and adventure while relieving any apprehension or misgivings the new person might have. Remember, anticipation is desirable; apprehension is not.

Congratulations . . .
and welcome to the Delaware County ARC. As a new employee you will be experiencing something unique called Vantage Point. You will spend your first day of employment in a role play exercise in which you will experience our program through the eyes of a program participant.

The Vantage Point Program has several purposes. We hope this experience will facilitate your empathy for the people being served. We also want you to feel what a proactive approach, positive atmosphere, and unified philosophy feels like on the receiving end of our services. We don't want you to just observe, but to actually feel what it is like to receive positive reinforcement and the attention that builds caring relationships and develops self-esteem.

In spite of our efforts, there may be times during the day when you may not feel particularly comfortable. We want you to recognize the cause of these feelings so that as an employee you can anticipate and avoid these conditions for the people we serve.

Another purpose for the Vantage Point Program is to accelerate your training. We take ongoing training very seriously and have found this program to be a key element. Your observations and experiences on this first day will help you better understand and appreciate subsequent training.

A final purpose of Vantage Point is to provide you an opportunity to take an active role in the ongoing training and development you will receive. We want you to critically observe what is going on around you. At the end of this experience you will be asked to bring any and all observations and concerns forward for discussion. These may not all be addressed on the first day, but they will give you and your supervisor clear avenues for follow-up in the days and weeks to come.

In preparation for this first day, we ask that you dress informally and that you bring a bag lunch. Your supervisor may have arranged for you to ride the bus to your designated program. If so, he/she will make the necessary arrangements and inform you of the specifics.

The last two things we ask you to bring are an open mind and enthusiasm. These will help make your experience exciting, educational and enjoyable. You will then have a truly unique vantage point from which to begin your experience at the Delaware County ARC.

Best wishes,
Jane Doe
Executive Director

A letter is one way to convey this message. Discussing at the time of hire or over the phone prior to the first day of employment can also be effective. In addition to this preparatory information, basic ground rules should be developed and explained at the very beginning of the Vantage Point experience.

Your organization will likely add other ground rules to the ones listed here that are necessary and unique to your particular setting.

Ground Rules:
•Stay within the role.
•Limit communication. Recall Jim being on the transport bus, strapped into place in his wheelchair. He tried to initiate small talk about his "real work" with the driver and the transport assistant. Both of them directed the conversation to how he felt in the chair and about his destination. They did talk about how cold everyone felt because it related to the role he was now playing.

•Cooperate with assigned tasks. When Jim was writing his left-handed letter, for instance, his mind began to wander. However, he recalled the talk Lynn and he had when he first sat down. She told him that even though staff hoped everyone enjoyed what they were doing, it was important they know each task was serious. Each one was designed to help them achieve the goals they set for themselves.
•Write down questions or impressions to discuss during the debriefing at the end of the day. Questions, concerns or perceptions left unattended may cause problems in the future.

Vantage Point Trainers

As stated earlier, trainers should be direct service professionals with strong work performance histories. Since they serve as models, facilitators, coaches and mentors, they should be chosen for their ability to put a positive face on your organization.

More importantly, they should possess a reservoir of caring and empathy, and be able to project these qualities sincerely. The trainer must offer challenges in a firm but not intimidating fashion yet remain supportive. Many of the exercises offer fun along with an opportunity for the trainer to induct this soon-to-be co-worker into the organization. A sense of humor is a valuable asset.

A trainer with a strong work performance history is not a rookie, but a person who is comfortable and patient with your service recipients. They should also be comfortable serving the dual role of direct service worker and trainer. These roles demand poise and experience. Your trainees will sense both, and they will relax and focus themselves.

Responsibilities and directions for Vantage Point trainers should be written down and may include the following.
•Stay within your role and help the trainees stay in theirs.
•Familiarize yourself with and follow all ground rules.

•Have all needed materials and supplies prepared in advance.

•Remember you are a model employee and we want the trainee to witness firsthand how excellent services are provided.

Vantage Point Coordinators

Coordinators assume primary responsibility for the training, coaching and supervision of trainers. Their other responsibilities include preliminary arrangements, scheduling, data collection and continually improving the quality of the Vantage Point experience. During the pilot period, any qualified individual may serve as the Vantage Point coordinator. However, when the pilot project is concluded and the program grows, it is best to have supervisory personnel serve as Vantage Point coordinators for the new employees they will be supervising.

Vantage Point coordinator responsibilities should also be clearly stated in writing. They may include the following.

•Make preparatory arrangements with new hires prior to their Vantage Point experience.

•Welcome the new hire on the Vantage Point day and introduce ground rules.

•Ensure that Vantage Point trainers are properly prepared, coached and supported.

•Resolve problems, concerns or difficulties that may arise during the Vantage Point day.

•Debrief both trainers and trainees. *(See the following section.)*

•Use feedback and information received during debriefing sessions to make recommendations for improving the program to the project team.

Reporting |

Debriefing

Debriefing a Vantage Point trainee will usually require between twenty and thirty minutes. Debriefing a Vantage Point trainer usually takes five to ten minutes. This process provides the opportunity to clarify or explain any part of the Vantage Point experience. It enables supervisors to clarify future expectations and it provides the input necessary to continually improve the program.

During debriefing, the trainee can ask all the questions that were either not allowed or not adequately addressed during the day. This allows for innocent misunderstandings or misconceptions to be cleared up. The discussion may also provide insight into his or her skills and abilities. For this reason, debriefings are best conducted by the new employee's immediate supervisor.

Data Collection and Written Feedback

Written feedback and collecting certain data may also be helpful. While verbal debriefing should be required, each Vantage Point team should determine what, if any, data needs to be collected. They should also determine if feedback should only occur verbally or whether certain information is best gathered in writing. It may be helpful to ask trainees to write a brief account of their impressions or to answer a survey prepared by the Vantage Point team.

Survey questions can be developed to evaluate whether particular goals were achieved as well as to determine if the trainee understood or benefited from the experience. Other data can be collected to address any number of concerns identified along the way. (For example, twelve years of data collection at the Delaware County ARC indicates that only one person out of hundreds who have experienced Vantage Point actually resigned at the end of the Vantage Point day).

Other questions to ask might include the following.

•Were you properly prepared/notified of the Vantage Point program prior to this morning?

•Was the Vantage Point experience realistic? Please explain.

•What are the strengths of the Vantage Point program?

•From what part of the day did you learn the most?

•How did you find the length of the day? The length of the experience?

•Did you ride the bus? Please describe your experience.

•Do you feel you have a better perspective on the people we serve?

•As a result of your Vantage Point experience, do you have a better understanding of what your future work will be like?

•Please explain in what ways the program did or did not work for you.

•Please list three suggestions for improving our Vantage Point program.

Conclusion |

A Vantage Point experience can have a profound and lasting impact on new employees. Accelerating training, and setting an enriched, dynamic tone for the employment relationship are hallmarks of an effective Vantage Point program. Use **Part 1** of this monograph to understand the benefits of such an experience and to inspire the creative energy needed to develop such a program. Then use the suggestions in **Part 2** to create a Vantage Point program that is fun, illuminating and insightful. In turn, new employees will be stimulated, encouraged and appreciative. Organizations that take such a dramatic, proactive approach will discover many advantages, but none more valued than the empathy, caring and trust that will result from this new perspective, this new Vantage Point.

About the Author |

George Suess has been employed by the Delaware County ARC in the Catskill Mountain Region of New York State for twenty-two years and has served as executive director for the past sixteen years. He also serves as senior consultant of its training division. He and other staff members of Delaware County ARC co-wrote *Shift Happens: Making the Shift to Proactive Behavior Management.*

As a consultant and trainer, Mr. Suess's goal is to inspire and motivate his audience to new paradigms of prevention and productivity. Focusing on values-based leadership and with an emphasis on common sense and hard work, he shows how individuals and organizations can make profound changes by taking small, practical steps towards improved performance and quality enhancement. "The problem," he often says, "is that common sense just isn't so common!"

Acknowledgments |

Jim Heikkinen, a freelance writer and all around good sport, took on his part of this assignment with a sense of adventure and wonder. We are also very grateful to our monograph team: Lucinda Brydon, Dr. Gerald Burday, Margaret Condon, Christine Fritzsch, Mark Gancasz, Sheri Hull, Molly Little, Rita McGee, Tammy Mullineaux, Barbara Rothenberg and Theresa Trotter.

We would also like to acknowledge and thank all the Delaware County ARC staff who invested loads of time and extremely productive energy over the last twelve years to make the Vantage Point Program one of excellence, fun and tradition. While there are far too many individuals to mention each one by name, we would be remiss not to thank veteran team members Christine Fritzsch, Sheri Hull, Barbara Rothenberg and Teresa Skinner, who have done so much since day one to make Vantage Point an essential element of the Delaware County ARC culture. Also, our first Vantage Point champion, David Denny, deserves our appreciation. He astutely pointed out, "You should only treat your employees like your consumers, if you treat your consumers well."

Steve Baker from High Tide Press caught the vision of this monograph from our first conversation and we are grateful for his encouragement and good sense. A host of volunteers donated their time and wisdom reviewing the many drafts that led up to this final work. We would like to acknowledge and thank them: Georgene Alberts, Linda Burns, Kathryn Casey, Gary Hull, Ty Little, Johanne Mazepa, Pam Moody, Christine Sears and Sharon Suess.

Last, and most certainly not least, our deepest appreciation goes to the hundreds of children and adults who, over the years, so willingly shared their lives with our new employees and taught them precious lessons we never could.